TRUST THE PROCESS

30 DAYS OF INSPIRATION TO ENRICH, ENHANCE, AND EMPOWER YOUR LIFE

LEANNE JONES

Trust the Process
30 Days of Inspiration to Enrich, Enhance, and Empower Your Life

ISBN: 978-0-9939974-0-2

ACKNOWLEDGEMENTS

To my parents and my sister, Abby, who are my biggest blessings. Thank you for being patient with me, supporting me, and celebrating my success. I promise to make you proud. Thank you to my encouraging best friend, Sierra, who supports any project I take on. A special thank you to my editor, Victoria Davis, for working with me on this project. Finally, to my supporters and readers, I honor and appreciate each of you.

This book is dedicated to the women who are committed to personal growth and embracing their life's experiences. I hope this book will change the way you see yourself and will help you to become an empowered woman. While on your journey, be open, take risks, and trust your inner sense to guide you. Remain patient through your transformation and **Trust the Process.**

CONTENTS

INTRODUCTION

Your journey of discovery will unfold and intensify each day as you read this book.

24 hours never seems to be enough time for all of the multitasking that women do in a day! It is in the nature of a woman to be hands on with everything. Sometimes, it just feels like we do not have a single moment to ourselves. Taking care of the home, working, and trying to make time for our families can feel like we're balancing several full time jobs. Amidst all of this, how can any woman keep her identity? How does she successfully become an empowered individual who is aware of her own needs? Is it just about "balancing" work and family? There are many women who do that these days. Have you ever wondered why it is so difficult for women to do something nice for themselves? Is it a lack of time and energy? That certainly seems like a reasonable excuse keeping in mind all of the things that women have lined up on the to-do list each day. The most important thing that women need for themselves is motivation to excel in every area of their lives.

If every day seems like a struggle to stay motivated, you probably don't realize how much you need a daily plan. Maybe you are unable to focus on keeping yourself motivated because you are overwhelmed with too much. Or maybe you're the complete opposite and feel like you've lost motivation because you don't have enough to do. Just staying motivated for one day will not help you find fulfillment in your life. You need to practice it over and over again until it becomes your ritual. If you are able to do that, you will definitely be able to see your own needs as a priority.

This book is a compilation of 30 things that you can do, one per day each month, to stay motivated and focused on a consistent basis. It is said that doing something consistently for 21 days becomes a habit, so let's make sure we can create a habit each day. This book is a compilation of simple, basic things that women ignore. If you are able to incorporate these things into your life, there is no reason why you will not be able to stay connected mentally, emotionally, and spiritually.

I hope this book empowers you to first see your life in a positive light, and then start making the necessary changes to live your life the way you always intended for it to be. It is time to let go of the boring routine and start creating moments that will help you see yourself as valuable. If nothing more, this book will help you make the necessary time for yourself as you learn about, and become, the new you. Now is the time to elevate your life and create an even better version of yourself. Let's begin...

DAY 1

Today is a great day to accomplish my goals. I have a positive vibe and I feel energized. I am aware of my priorities and tasks that I need to complete. I am at the top of my game! I have full control of my emotions and will think positive thoughts, set a goal for the day, and aim to achieve it.

Set the Day up for Success

"Four things for success: work and pray, think and believe."
– Norman Peale

Today is the start of your journey to becoming a new you. I encourage you to start Day 1 on a Sunday. Chances are you've had a busy weekend and you probably don't feel like going back to work tomorrow. The weekend is just a small break from all the hard work that we put into our homes and our careers. So, a Sunday is the perfect day to plan the week out. Have you ever wondered why Mondays seem so depressing? Why does it feel so impossible sometimes to get out of bed? Part of it is the lack of preparation for Monday before it comes. One of the easiest ways to regain control over the "Monday blues" is to get ready for the new week on Sunday night. Yes, it's possible! Since you know that the next day is a workday, prepare for it. It is a great idea to get all of your things organized the night before. You can prepare your lunch for the next day, lay out your outfits for the week, and even plan out your social events. That way, when you start your day on Monday, and especially when you get to work, you won't feel so out of control with all of the things that need to get done.

Another helpful tip is, have a light dinner on Sunday night. We tend to binge on Sunday nights. While that can be fun, what this does is make you lazy the next morning. The reason you can't pull yourself out of bed on a Monday morning is because Sunday night's dinner and late night snacks are weighing you down.

Once you've had a balanced meal for Sunday and taken some time to prepare for the week, get some extra sleep. Saturday is good for all your late night adventures but it's a good idea to go to bed early on a Sunday night. Also, try not to fall asleep watching TV or a movie. Instead, try reading a book or find something that allows you to settle your mind. This can range from listening to soft music to exercising. The goal is to keep each morning as relaxed as possible by ending the previous day in a relaxed state of mind. Usually, mornings are rushed and really stressful, so it is also a good idea to set the alarm a little earlier than usual. When you wake up early, you give yourself enough time to incorporate a morning routine. A cup of detoxifying tea or lemon water before breakfast and a short morning workout or 30-minute stretch routine before a shower can be a great jump start. Now you have the time and energy you need to look good because you feel good. You should pick out a great outfit, do your hair and make-up just the way you want it, and walk out the door feeling ready for the day.

Helpful Habits

* Create morning rituals to keep you productive all day.

* Stretch or exercise, then have a healthy smoothie. It's easy and energizing!

* Pick at least one thing you'd like to accomplish each day to feel like the day was a success.

DAY 2

I will make sure my body gets all the exercise it needs. I will not waste my time complaining about body aches and fatigue. Choosing to stay fit is my way of loving myself. I will start a workout plan and commit to spending at least 30 minutes a day focusing on physical fitness.

Focus on Physical Fitness

"Physical fitness is not only one of the most important keys to a healthy body, it is the basis of dynamic and creative intellectual activity."
– John F. Kennedy

Finding a great fitness routine is a good way to stay motivated. The right exercise program will help you start/end your day with a rush of adrenaline and endorphins. Endorphins or "happy hormones" help keep you mentally relaxed. They will help you focus and feel better about all that you need to get done today.

Taking care of yourself physically is one important way of showing that you care about how you feel inside out. One thing that motivates women is looking good! When you spend time working on your physique, you will begin to see your skin glow. As a result, over time, you will start to feel more confident in who you are.

As good as getting into shape sounds, the biggest struggle for most of us is getting started and sticking with it. The visit to the gym is always pushed to next week or the first of the next month. And, let's not forgot about all of those New

Year resolutions we make to join the gym each year, promising ourselves and others that we're really going to do it. But today, on the second day of your motivation regime, make the commitment that you're going to do your absolute best to get your body into shape.

Women tend to ignore this important part of their lives and our biggest excuse is "I don't have the time." However, you can definitely take a few minutes or an hour for yourself each day. Find a friend who's willing to meet you at the gym 2–3 times a week. You can even get your family (sisters, cousins, etc.) involved. You do not have to necessarily workout the same time every day and you don't always have to do it alone. Identify your struggle with getting into shape, set a goal for yourself, get a personal trainer, and link up with your close girlfriends. Be creative, make it fun, and do whatever it takes for you to start and complete your goal.

Having a fitness routine is not just good for your body, but equally important for your mind. Having some dedicated time to yourself gives you another positive way to stay healthy, relieve stress, boost your energy, and increase your chances of living a longer, more productive life. Don't think about fitness in a negative way. This is another way for you to dedicate some time for yourself each day. When you are working out, try to relieve yourself from any worries and allow your mind to be free and focus solely on you!

Imagine seeing yourself one month from now, then 6 months from now. When the compliments start to come in, you'll be so proud of the day you started taking better care of your body. Everyone will tell you how great you are looking on the outside and you'll be feeling just as good on the inside. Keep in mind that Day 2 is not set up to be the one day that you work out and then stop. Today is the day you make your commitment and keep going. After you experience the difference, you will be on your way to physical and mental wellness for a lifetime!

Helpful Habits

* Reflect on unhealthy decisions that you are making or need to change.

* Decide on a workout routine and healthy diet plan and commit to it.

* Have a fitness journal or calendar that includes a daily log of the following: day of the week, water consumed, meals, and workout (optional: hours of sleep, energy level [high/low], and stress level [high/low]).

DAY 3

I have a great life and a lot to be thankful for. I am passionate about my dreams and desires, and am in pursuit of happiness that I can experience in my own life and share with others.

Find More Reasons to Be Grateful

"Cultivate the habit of being grateful for every good thing that comes to you, and to give thanks continuously. And because all things have contributed to your advancement, you should include all things in your gratitude."
– Ralph Waldo Emerson

With the chaos of our busy lives, it's easy to be ungrateful at times. We are spoiled by material comfort and living a life full of excess. We sometimes take things for granted and feel entitled to certain types of treatment, often forgetting that being grateful allows us to keep a positive perspective. Expressing gratitude reminds us that blessings come in all forms and by being grateful, we will become conscious of the many blessings we have already received.

Today, keep in mind that gratitude is an attitude that needs to be cultivated and nurtured. Don't take gracious acts of others for granted or act as if you are entitled to others helping or supporting you. Express gratitude from a humble place within and develop a prosperity consciousness. Be a woman who constantly looks for opportunities to express gratitude.

Acknowledge your blessings and treat others with appreciation and be thankful with an open heart.

Helpful Habits

* As you go about your day, look for ways to express gratitude.

* Give thanks willingly with an open heart.

* Create a "blessings jar". Write down the things you are grateful for and read over them every once in a while as a reminder of how blessed you are.

DAY 4

Today, regardless of what others define success as, I will redefine my own meaning of success and pursue it on my own terms.

Redefine Success

"Define success on your own terms, achieve it by your own rules and build a life you're proud to live."
– Anne Sweeny

Society and our culture has done its part to present images of success that equate to things such as reaching a certain level of formal education, obtaining a certain amount of money, gaining a particular social status, and of course, having different types of material things. By doing this, it sets us up to be in constant pursuit of these things. Today, empower yourself by reframing your thoughts from what success is perceived as, and instead, define it in your own way. For you, success can be clearly identifying your life's purpose, having nourishing and fulfilling friendships, or even establishing a new relationship. Above all, living a life that brings you joy and happiness is what is most important.

Helpful Habits

* Don't compare yourself to the success of others.

* Be happy for others when they succeed or do well at something.

* Frame your own future.

DAY 5

Today, I will be good to myself. I will compliment myself and speak only positive things about who I am. I will be patient in areas where I am growing and improving, and be proud of myself for things that I have accomplished.

Be Kind to Yourself

"A girl should be two things: who and what she wants."
– CoCo Chanel

When was the last time you did something nice for yourself? For some of us, when was the last time we even said something nice about ourselves or were able to receive a kind compliment that someone gave us? Sadly, a lot of women spend more time complaining about their shortcomings than celebrating their strengths. We always tell ourselves what we need to change physically, how inefficient we are, or how much we are "not like someone else". The only person you were created to be is, you. It's time to start loving and appreciating who you are.

We have all heard that greatness is achieved only when we push ourselves harder; but sometimes, we overdo it. You don't have to be the prettiest, smartest, most successful woman in the world. Nor do you have to force yourself to be perfect. Take the day to do something different. Sleep in late. Eat whatever you want. Don't obsess about the way your hair looks. Don't compare yourself to the models you see in magazines or on social media. Instead, find something that you absolutely love about yourself and hold on to it all day long. If you feel overwhelmed or compelled to push yourself in the wrong direction, take a moment to gather your thoughts. This will take some work, but overtime you will learn that the kindness you show to yourself is equally important as the kindness you show to others.

Helpful Habits

* Don't force yourself to be perfect.

* Learn to accept yourself just the way you are.

* Be patient, loving, and gentle with yourself each day.

DAY 6

Today, I will find three things that I have never done before and discover ways to do each of them.

Do New Things

*"If you want something new, you have to stop
doing something old."*
– Peter F. Drucker

See today as an opportunity to try and focus on new experiences. Do you want to take a trip somewhere that reflects your passions; or how about cooking something exotic? You can choose anything you desire, but you must make sure that you have never experienced it before. It is important for you to get out of your comfort zone and be spontaneous!

Why is this so important, you ask? Well, new experiences are extremely motivating. They tell you that you are able to take on challenges and live up to them even when you have no clue about what you are trying to do. Trying new things gives you the confidence to accept new challenges that may come your way. But most importantly, trying something new is fun! It is a break from a rather boring routine that you probably have set for yourself by now. If you are really looking for motivation, there is definitely nothing better than doing something entirely different from what you are used to doing on a regular basis.

It has been observed that people who are successful always engage in activities that they have not experienced before. Even the simplest of tasks can have an impact. Don't shy awayfrom doing something new and don't be lazy about it either! This is your chance to learn. It is also your chance to gather new experiences and improve on your knowledge. What are you waiting for? Make that list now!

Helpful Habits

* Make sure your ideas and wants always match your actions. If you think of an idea to do something new, do it!

* Take time to develop and master unknown skills by facing new challenges. Get out of your comfort zone!

DAY 7

Today, I will devote time for myself.

Take the Day Off

"Rest is not idleness, and to lie sometimes on the grass under trees on a summer's day, listening to the murmur of the water, or watching the clouds float across the sky, is by no means a waste of time."
– John Lubbock

You have been on your feet all week ripping and running. Let today be the one day of the week that you relax. Pamper yourself, perhaps. Let all the chores take a back seat. Since today is your day off, grab a movie, stock up on the snacks, longue around, and be at peace. Have someone else do the cooking or even better, opt for delivery or takeout. Do not obsess about anything. Yes, the house may need to be cleaned, the dishes may need to be washed, the laundry could be piling up, but it can all wait. You can get back to your regular "superwoman" routine tomorrow. It is your day to sleep in late, enjoy a cup of coffee with a good book, go shopping, or do whatever you want to do (even if it means doing nothing). Reward yourself. You deserve it!

Helpful Habits

* Take time to gather your thoughts and relieve any
  feelings of stress.

* Allow yourself to get some extra rest and relaxation.

* Take a long, hot bath or simply do nothing.

Notes and Ideas

Date: _____

_____

_____

_____

_____

_____

_____

_____

_____

_____

_____

_____

_____

_____

_____

Plan of Action

Date: ――――――――――

_____

_____

_____

_____

_____

_____

_____

_____

_____

_____

_____

_____

_____

DAY 8

Today, there are several things that I have been putting off that I
need to do! All the small, odd tasks that keep popping up when
I am in the middle of an important project will be taken care of.
No more procrastinating.

Get Rid of the Clutter

*"The purpose of order is to increase productivity
and create comfort."*
– Unknown

What are the nagging tasks that you've been avoiding lately? We all have things around the home as well as at work that we need to do, but we keep putting it off. Did you forget to reply to an email? Or maybe you haven't finished cleaning out your closet yet. Are you still avoiding the task of organizing that one messy desk drawer at work that's driving you crazy? Is the filing cabinet still cluttered with old files that need to be recycled? Even though some of these tasks are extremely mundane, they can pile up into a heap before you know it. The clutter around us can go from being small and tolerant to so overwhelming that we do our best to ignore that it's there.

Today, create a to-do list and establish a plan to get one thing done at a time. When certain things in your life get out of order, it can cause confusion and become demotivating; but if you make it a point to get them done and out of the way, it can actually help alter your mood tremendously. Once you cross that last item off your list, you will feel a sense of peace and the space around you will feel less chaotic and stressful.

Helpful Habits

* Prioritize and organize your life. Make it simple for yourself by doing these two simple steps: plan and perform.

* Turn down requests that will interfere with your goals and priorities.

DAY 9

Today I will be in tune with myself. I will be present to my emotions, moods, and the effect I have on others around me. I will be more aware of my body changes, my habits, behaviors, thoughts, interactions, and the words I speak.

Be Present and Aware

*"The present moment is filled with joy and happiness. If
you are attentive, you will see it."*
– Thích Nhất Hạnh

B eing more present with yourself is the best way to help you live in the moment. It also allows you to be more thankful for the moments of bliss that bless your life! Sometimes you just have to stop, close your eyes, and allow yourself to move into a calm and relaxed state. Settle down comfortably and enjoy several seconds of peace while focusing on the current moment. Try not to always think so far ahead!

Today, focus on being more self-aware when it comes to your feelings. If you catch yourself in a bad mood or with an attitude, check yourself and adjust it. If you find yourself in an angry state, don't allow it to shut you down or to steer you off your path. A great life lesson to practice is to treat emotions, such as anger for example, lightly. Examine your anger and learn from it. All of your moods, emotions, habits, and behaviors either empower or deprive you. The choice is yours!

Helpful Habits

* Give yourself permission to explore and express your emotions lightly and from the heart.

 * Live in the moment!

* Don't overthink the present or the future. Learn to be at peace.

DAY 10

Today, I will send out messages of love to the people I care about and tell them how much I love them.

Tell the People You Love How Much They Mean to You

"Don't wait until it's too late to tell someone how much you love and how much you care about them, because when they're gone, no matter how loud you shout and cry, they won't hear you anymore."
– Unknown

We often find ourselves struggling when it comes to telling people how much we actually care about them. Most often, this is because we take those same people for granted. When you tell someone that you love and appreciate them, you feel immense joy. You will find that expressing love makes you happy. Of course, when your loved ones reciprocate the love, you feel even more happiness. Simple messages of love create positive thoughts and emotions, and we all need that.

The truth is, it actually takes courage to tell someone how you really feel about them. Is it difficult for you to tell your parents, spouse, kids, or even your best friends that you are glad they are a part of your life? They are constantly praying for you and supporting you. Knowing this is the biggest moral boost. Since the people around you may find it hard to express their love too, take the initiative. Don't put it off another day. Write an email, send a text, or pick up the phone and tell the people you love how much they mean to you!

Helpful Habits

* Reach out to close family and friends to tell them how much you love them.

* Notice how good it feels to express your love to the people you care about.

DAY 11

Today, I will go out of my way to give a compliment to someone and brighten their day.

Give Someone a Compliment

"Do your little bit of good where you are; it's those little bits of good put together that overwhelm the world."
– Desmond Tutu

Make today about someone else, even if that person is a total stranger. Find someone around you who may be having a bad day and give them a kind compliment to cheer them up. Yes, there are people who we may find it very hard to give compliments to. This often includes the people we live with or see at work every day. Tell your spouse he looks nice today or if you have children, tell them that you're proud of them and reward them for something good they've done recently. Compliment your boss or your co-worker on a new outfit or hairdo. It's a small gesture that could make someone's day.

When you compliment people around you, it makes the atmosphere more pleasant and enjoyable; and if you do it when you first see them, it can easily set the tone for the rest of their day. We all have things going on in our lives that may bring us down, but today help build someone else's self-confidence whenever opportunities arise. If not by a compliment, then share some enthusiasm and optimism with those around you. It's almost impossible to make someone else's day without making your own in the process.

Helpful Habits

* Enhance your conversation with others by sincerely complimenting them.

* Pay it forward. Treat others the way you want to be treated.

* People appreciate you when you are kind and genuine. Never miss the opportunity to be that for someone.

DAY 12

Today, I am letting go of anything that is holding me back. I choose to look ahead to the amazing things in store for me rather than hold on to past hurts, memories, or things that are no longer of use to me.

Let Go and Trust That Everything Is Going to Be Alright

"Some people believe holding on and hanging in there are signs of great strength. However, there are times when it takes much more strength to know when to let go and then do it."
– Ann Landers

We all go through unpleasant situations. While these situations are meant to teach us important life lessons, they are not designed to hold us back and keep us trapped in our past. There are many things that can keep us from looking ahead and visualizing the future. This can be small memorabilia that remind us of a past relationship, or memories of a difficult time we experienced. Letting go of these unpleasant memories can really help you look forward to the better things that await you. Today, find the strength to forgive yourself and others so that it no longer has the power to weigh you down. Any tangible things from your past that brings back negative emotions should be on your list of things to get rid of today. Do not ponder over it or try to convince yourself to keep these items lying around. Even though that item represented something good in the past, it's time to let it go and move on. You deserve to find the peace you need in order to live your life and enjoy it, present and future. Say goodbye to the past, learn to let go, and set your spirit free!

Helpful Habits

* Try speaking a let-it-go mantra in your head and feel the internal release of what you are holding on to. Do it until you are okay with the outcome and feel at peace.

* Release some unnecessary things out of your life in order to evolve.

DAY 13

Today, I will pick a new book and start reading it. I will try to read something informative or inspirational daily. I will challenge myself intellectually and embrace what I learn.

Read a Good Book

"The more that you read, the more things you will know. The more that you learn, the more places you'll go."
– Dr. Seuss

When was the last time you read a good book? If you are an avid reader, you probably know how enjoyable reading is. But if reading is something you tend to shy away from, you are missing out. Not only is reading fundamental, it truly is a way to relax, unwind, and stimulate the mind. There are so many benefits to reading books. Reading helps you stay alert and in some cases, a good book will challenge you to change, or even motivate you to keep pushing forward.

Books are such a powerful tool and some of us don't realize this until we get more serious about our life's purpose. The books you read can shape you into becoming a better version of yourself and will help to open your mind and ignite your gifts and talents. Once you find a good book, be prepared to expand your vision and accept any strategies or lessons you take in. Learning new things through reading will make your life more interesting and exciting. Take time to select and read useful books whether your preference is fiction or nonfiction. There's something out there for everyone.

Helpful Habits

* When reading, use highlighters, bookmarks, and a pen to jot down your thoughts.

* Treat reading like a mini escape. Try to get in a relaxing setting in order to focus and be more productive.

* Read books that will enhance what it is you're passionate about.

DAY 14

Today is all about family. I have been so busy reaching my goals and making things happen for myself that I may have neglected my family lately. I will make it a point to get the whole family together for some quality time.

Spend the Day With Your Family

"Love your family. Spend time, be kind and serve one another. Make no room for regrets. Tomorrow is not promised and today is short." – Unknown

In the daily attempts to keep our lives on track, we sometimes forget to make time for our families. As women, we're wearing so many different hats at one time — student, wife, mom, supervisor, etc. It's important that we make time for our family as often as we can. Being around your loved ones can really be revitalizing and uplifting. When you are with your family, you can be yourself and escape from your hectic life.

Never hesitate to express your love towards your family while you are in their presence. Honor them and never put them down. Love your family enough to make personal improvements on yourself that way when you're spending time together you can laugh more and create a stronger bond even if you all have different personalities. When spending time with your family, let them express themselves. Take the time to talk to them about their feelings and try your best to support them. Think of new ways you can show your love to them during quality time. If nothing more, today will be a day well spent amidst people who really love and care about you just as much as you do them.

Helpful Habits

* Allow spending time with family to bring out the best in you.

* Have fun with your family. Make each moment count.

* Tell your family members how much you love them!

Notes and Ideas

Date: _____

_____

_____

_____

_____

_____

_____

_____

_____

_____

_____

_____

_____

_____

_____

Plan of Action

Date: _____

_____

_____

_____

_____

_____

_____

_____

_____

_____

_____

_____

_____

_____

_____

_____

_____

DAY 15

Today, I will not take myself too seriously and will give myself room to make mistakes. I need to first stop being so hard on myself.

Laugh at Yourself

"I laugh at myself. I don't take myself completely seriously..."
– Madonna

Have you ever felt completely burdened with a mistake you made? Suppose you stuttered over your words while making an important presentation. Or what if you slipped and fell in front of a crowd of people? What would you do, never go out in public again? Well, there's actually an easier way to handle those mishaps that occur in our lives. Your task for today is to make it a point to laugh at the mistakes you make. Even if you are so embarrassed by a mistake that you want to fall into a hole in the ground; laugh it off.

As women, we are always internally striving to be perfect. Sometimes our whole life revolves around the image of perfection that we have created for ourselves. We need to be impeccably dressed, articulate at all times, and completely in control of every situation that we find ourselves in. Stop putting yourself through all of this and remember that you are human just like everyone else. Until you stop stressing yourself out about everything around you being perfect, you will be affected by the smallest things that go wrong in your day. When you take yourself too seriously, you are unable to let go of your mistakes. Most of us tend to carry a big weight on our shoulders, so even the slightest inconvenience makes us question everything around us. One small failure and we are convinced that we are good for nothing. One hiccup along the way and we just give up and decide that success is not for us. When you lose the ability to laugh at yourself, you tend to overthink everything. The day you can embrace life as it comes, good and bad, you will learn to live in the freedom of accepting your imperfections and accept yourself just the way you are, flaws and all.

Helpful Habits

* Learn to laugh it off!

* Don't take things too seriously. Give yourself a break!

* Don't overthink or overanalyze. Live in the freedom of being yourself.

DAY 16

Today, I am evolving, maturing, and changing continuously in spite of my past or current struggles. I will not resist growth. My life is a journey, not a destination, and I will continue to move forward.

Embrace Your Struggles

"We grow because we struggle, we learn and overcome."
– R.C. Allen

Embracing your struggles simply means learning from what you have been through, or may be currently going through. It is about learning all of the lessons that life is teaching you and becoming a better version of yourself while creating a better future. Allow every obstacle thrown your way to build your inner strength and character. Pick yourself up and strive to be a strong, bold, unstoppable, and powerful woman.

When it comes to your struggles, be real with yourself and don't try to pretend that you have it all together. Be honest, transparent, and trust that you will no longer have to live in denial out of shame and embarrassment. Living within your own truth of what you go through will set you free. Be open minded in order to be empowered to make necessary changes. It has been said that "change happens when the pain of staying the same is greater than the pain of change." Ask yourself, what needs to change in my world?

Helpful Habits

* Reflect on your past struggles and realize what lessons you have learned from them that made you a better person.

* Remember that your life is a journey, and the lessons you are taught along the way from your struggles are the most important.

DAY 17

Today, I will identify and acknowledge my fears. Whether big or small, I am prepared to face and overcome them one by one.

Face Your Fears

"One of the greatest discoveries a man makes, one of his great surprises, is to find he can do what he was afraid he couldn't' do."
– Henry Ford

The only thing that holds us back from achieving anything is fear. When doubt and fear get in our way, we are distracted from living a happy life. Today, list all your fears and begin making an effort to think about all the things that are holding you back from being the incredible woman you are. Be determined to no longer allow your fears to be a mental block towards your success.

It is normal to have concerns, but you cannot allow yourself to be controlled or hindered by constant worry and fear. The most important thing to understand is whether or not your fears have any basis or if you are amplifying them in your mind. No matter where you are on your journey, there will always be risks involved. Whether it is a decision to move to another state, accepting a new job, or just making day-to-day changes in your routine. If you are only worried about the risks and the repercussions, you will never be able to move ahead.

Take your time and really think about this, but also be honest with yourself. Even if some of your fears seem completely irrational, write them down. Anything that is stopping you from progressing needs to be eliminated. Once you face it, you can overcome it and achieve great things.

Helpful Habits

* Change your mindset when it comes to fear and see it as an opportunity to grow.

* Boldly take control over your fears!

* First acknowledge your fears, then overcome them.

DAY 18

Today, I am making a conscious effort to grow!

Ready to Grow!

"You are confined only by the walls you build yourself."
– Andrew Murphy

Many believe that we are designed for evolving. Interestingly, so many people are resistant to doing so. Settling, instead of expanding, is choosing to be stagnate. Picture your life as consistently unfolding, and how you choose to move through the process is up to you. When it comes to your personal growth, strive to live your life to the fullest and not be afraid to push through uncomfortable situations or challenges. If you choose a path of resistance your life can easily become boring and too comfortable.

Growth is a process. One of the most important things a woman must have in order to propel onward, and to keep from slowing down, is self-motivation. Self-motivation is the force that will push you to do things that you desire. It is a life skill that we need to have, especially when working on things that have to do with our personal development.

The combination of growth and motivation will drive you to achieve your goals and feel better about the overall quality of your life. Understanding and embracing the need for growth will allow you to gain full control over your life.

Helpful Habits

* Self-motivation will assist you in your personal growth process.

* Be confident in your growth and learn to find a balance between your personal and professional goals.

DAY 19

Today, I will acknowledge the hard work that I have done and congratulate myself on recent professional and personal achievements in my life.

Acknowledge Your Accomplishments

"Success is not measured by what you accomplish but by the opposition you have encountered, and the courage with which you have maintained the struggle against overwhelming odds."
– Orison Swett Marden

Have you ever failed to acknowledge the things you have accomplished recently? Your achievements tell you how far you have come. Although you should always be striving to do more, this does not mean you should overlook the positive steps you have made to get to where you are now. We tend to support everyone else around us when they have accomplished something but we rarely give ourselves the credit we deserve when we do something great.

Make a note of every milestone you set for yourself that you have already reached this year. Tell yourself that if you have come this far, you can go anywhere. Let nothing hold you back. When you can, take the time to reflect on your accomplishments. Judge yourself based on the things that you have succeeded at, not the things that did not work out well for you. These achievements are not always career or academic related. Recognize the fact that you are a great wife, friend, mom, daughter, and all around, a wonderful person. Think about the many challenges you have overcome in spite of all that has been thrown your way. Sometimes, your greatest accomplishment is knowing when you could have given up, but you didn't. That's a lot to be proud of.

Helpful Habits

* Acknowledge all of your accomplishments despite how small they may seem.

* Be proud of yourself!

* Keep setting goals for yourself along the way. Let every accomplishment inspire you to aim for the next goal.

DAY 20

Today, I will get out of the house and spend some time being one with nature.

Get Some Fresh Air

*"The clearest way into the Universe is through
a forest wilderness."*
– John Muir

When was the last time you took a vacation or just went for a nice, quiet walk? You deserve a break. In fact, you need it! When you are feeling unmotivated, overwhelmed, stressed out, or just having a bad week, it is your body's way of telling you that you are doing too much. You need to slow down and get away for a while. Don't wait for all your friends or family to join you. Go with anyone who has the time. If you feel like it is too much work getting others to join you, go alone. There is no better way to relax than to spend some time with yourself enjoying nature.

This time away does not have to be a fancy getaway. Think of it is an opportunity to unwind and collect your thoughts. Find a quiet and calm location like a park in your area, the nearest beach, or a safe, quiet place where you can take a walk. The idea is to be in a place free from phone calls, noise, and the chaos of your busy schedule. When your atmosphere is calm and quiet, you will be able to align your mind and your spirit.

Nature is a great way to reconnect with your inner self. Allow your senses to be rejuvenated. Take in the beauty of the sights and sounds around you. You need to be in a space that is entirely free from all the worries and trouble in your life. You need some fresh air!

Helpful Habits

* Always make some time to go outside and clear your mind.

* Learn to become one with nature.

* Find quiet, calm places where you can think clearly and escape the "noise" of your daily routine.

DAY 21

Today, I will focus on living out my purpose by first identifying what my purpose is.

Live Purposefully

*"Efforts and courage are not enough without
purpose and direction."*
– John F Kennedy

There will always be people who are not on the same page as you, but what matters most is your faithfulness to fulfilling your own purpose in life. Each of us has something unique about ourselves that defines why we are here on earth. Live authentically by staying true to who you are, and be bold enough to be yourself, unapologetically. Work on having complete clarity when it comes to your purpose and no matter how long it takes you to discover it, never neglect it.

Set an example worth following but don't focus solely on getting other people to follow you. Understand what really matters and remember that as you continue to grow, life is going to continue to test you then teach you. Living out your purpose allows you to take advantage of every moment of the day. As you identify your purpose, you learn who you really are and your life starts to have meaning. Your purpose works *for* you, not against you. Get to the root of what you believe you were placed here to do. Once you have identified that, start applying ways to grow in your purpose each day. This helps to ensure that you are consistently moving in the right direction.

Helpful Habits

* Match your purpose with what it is you're truly passionate about.

* Connect with your natural gifts and talents to enhance your purpose.

Notes and Ideas

Date: _____

_____

_____

_____

_____

_____

_____

_____

_____

_____

_____

_____

_____

_____

Plan of Action

Date: ———————————

———————————————————————

———————————————————————

———————————————————————

———————————————————————

———————————————————————

———————————————————————

———————————————————————

———————————————————————

———————————————————————

———————————————————————

———————————————————————

———————————————————————

———————————————————————

———————————————————————

———————————————————————

DAY 22

Today, I will make a vision board. It will be a precise compilation of the most important goals that I have set for myself. I know what my dreams are and I have defined them properly; now I will illustrate them to create a strong visual tool for myself.

Make a Vision Board

"To accomplish great things we must first dream, then visualize, then plan... believe... act!"
– Alfred A. Montapert

A vision board is a compilation of all the things that you want to achieve. When you have a clear visual aid to see what you want to do with your life, it is much easier to make progress. A vision board is like a road map that tells you where you are headed. It is a representation of all the goals and dreams that you have created for yourself and a great way to stay motivated.

Before you set out to make your vision board, collect several images, your favorite inspirational quotes, scriptures, or even funny caricatures. Whatever connects with you that will motivate you each time you look at your board, add it. These images should represent not only your goals, but also the things you would like to experience in your life. This process can be a lot of fun. Start with a one-year plan. As the year goes on, expand your vision board to a three-year plan, and then eventually to a five-year plan. Don't forget to include pictures of yourself on your vision board as well. Keep it neat and easy on the eyes. Clarity and simplicity will help you focus better on your future.

Helpful Habits

* Be clear and specific about what it is you truly desire for you life when putting together your vision board.

* Consider a vision board for your specific goals and an inspirational board for quotes and images that inspire you or make you feel good.

DAY 23

Today, I will properly nurture the relationships I have with those who genuinely want the best for me. I will be wise and only surround myself with people who celebrate the good things about me, help me to stay positive, and are optimistic about my future..

Surround Yourself With Good People

"When you're surrounded by people who share a passionate commitment around a common purpose, anything is possible."
– Howard Schultz

One of the most important aspects of your life is being cautious about who you invest your time and energy into. Be sure you are surrounding yourself with people who consistently add value to your life. Today, evaluate what types of friends you have established. Make sure these people have a similar mindset and core values. No two people are exactly the same. It is important that you interact with all types of individuals. However, it is important that those in your closest circle are invested in growing, maturing, and bettering themselves just as you are. These are the types of friends who can give you fresh perspectives to help enrich your life.

Who you are around versus those who are always wanting to be around you makes a big difference in the types of things you talk about, the kinds of activities you engage in, and where your focus is. Who you associate with can sometimes affect how you feel and their attitudes can unconsciously become your own. Don't allow negative people around you, as it will only lead to demotivation. If you keep the right people in your life and separate yourself from those who are not helping you grow, this will lift your spirits and outlook on almost everything.

Helpful Habits

* Surround yourself with people who pull you up, not those who pull you down.

* Purge when necessary! Go through your social media accounts, contact list in your phone and email, and disconnect from anyone who does not serve a positive purpose in your life.

DAY 24

Today, I will focus on ways that I can strengthen my body and mind. I will think clearly and be free of worry.

Rejuvenation Day

"Every person needs to take one day away. A day in which one consciously separates the past from the future. Jobs, family, employers, and friends can exist one day without any one of us, and if our egos permit us to confess, they could exist eternally in our absence. Each person deserves a day away in which no problems are confronted, no solutions searched for. Each of us needs to withdraw from the cares which will not withdraw from us."
– Maya Angelou

Why do we feel unmotivated or not up to par sometimes? It is because we stretch ourselves thin by taking on more than we can handle. As women, one of our biggest problems is that we take everything too seriously. Whether it is our home or our work, we feel the need to be totally present and hands on nonstop. Our minds become cluttered with so many thoughts that we get burned out and shut down. It is important that you take regular time away from technology and the media to ground yourself and come back to your center. Remember your mind, body, and spirit need your attention too.

I urge you to take a day of rejuvenation. De-stress and reconnect with yourself. This is truly your time to unwind and get your thoughts in place. It is important for everyone to take that one day to allow your mind to rest. After you renew your mind, you will feel much better when you get back to your regular routine. You will be able to organize your thoughts clearly and prioritize the things that need to get done. You will realize that you were so caught up with everything else that you forgot to pay attention to you.

Helpful Habits

* Don't be a workaholic. Take time to let your mind rest.

* Push away unnecessary stress and drama.

* Keep a daily journal to express thoughts and ideas clearly.

DAY 25

Today I am going to do something to pamper myself. I deserve it!

Pamper Yourself

"You yourself, as much as anybody in the entire universe, deserve your love and affection."
– Gautama Buddha

Have you ever noticed how easy it is to do nice things for others, yet when it comes to doing things for yourself you almost feel a sense of guilt? Spend today pampering and loving yourself completely.

When we look at ourselves, we often see all of our shortcomings and imperfections. This is one of the main reasons why it is so hard for us to love ourselves. Start the day in a peaceful state. Stand in front of the mirror and stare at your reflection. Do you love yourself? Are you taking the time you need to care for yourself or are you burnt out from loving everyone else? Pick something that you really want to indulge in and go for it. Are you feeling stiff and tired? If so, a massage is a good option. If you feel like your hair is a mess, how about making an appointment with your stylist for a new, sassy haircut? While you're at it, treat yourself to a manicure and pedicure. You work hard and you've been going nonstop. It's time for you to pamper yourself!

When you take time to relax and rejuvenate, you will find that you become a happier person. The better you feel about yourself, the better you feel about life. Be selfish today and allow yourself to take in the love that you need and deserve. At the end of the day when you look in the mirror again, you will cherish the way you feel and see yourself after a day of pampering. It will do wonders for you!

Helpful Habits

* Always make time to do something nice for yourself.

* Put together a pampering kit for yourself that includes candles, essential oils, natural bubble baths, and body sponges. Have it ready for when you need it.

DAY 26

Today, I want to look my absolute best. I will add to my
confidence through the way I dress, my beauty regimen,
and the way I wear my hair and accessories.

Update Your Image and Enhance Your Wardrobe

"Seeing, feeling, thinking, believing - these are the stages of how we change our style on the outside and our self-image on the inside."
– Stacey London

Develop a constant routine of looking your very best. When you dress well, this can also make you feel better about yourself. The way you feel on the inside should radiate to your outward appearance, so it is important to always feel fabulous and confident from the inside out as best you can. Start doing this by getting rid of any negative, unhelpful thoughts or attitudes you may have about enhancing your personal image. For instance, get rid of the "I don't care about the way I look" attitude, or the "It's not worth the energy" types of thoughts. The reality is, your appearance easily influences your emotions and the key is to always work from the inside out. Improve your inner confidence and mindset about your physical appearance. Tell yourself "I am a beautiful, confident woman" then show that confidence on the outside!

Helpful Habits

* Gain knowledge of what is currently fashionable yet allow your own style to shine through. Look at recent fashion magazines or follow fashion icons and blogs and see the latest trends.

* At the end of each season, do and inventory of your closet. Donate the clothes you can no longer wear, then reward yourself and go shopping. Try to add pieces that you wouldn't normally wear to spice up your new wardrobe. Be creative!

DAY 27

I am a perfect reflection of my beautiful soul. I accept myself deeply and completely. Loving myself unconditionally is essential and I have confidence in my ability to do whatever I set my mind to.

Love Yourself

"The most powerful relationship you will ever have is the relationship with yourself."
– Steve Maraboli

L oving you and practicing self-care is never a selfish act. Loving and caring for yourself as a woman is an extremely important factor in order to nurture and renew your mind and body before attempting to do the same for others. You can only give away what you have. This is why practicing self-care first can really serve you and others in a positive way.

Instead of constantly feeling stressed or worn out, operate from a place of renewal. Charge your inner self like you do your cell phone. If you don't re-charge, you won't be able to function and do what you need to do! Once you are taken care of, you are then present, available, and able to meet all of your responsibilities, commitments, and priorities.

A self-care approach when it comes to your life is always a win-win situation. This is because when you take care of yourself first, everything and everybody from family, work, relationships, and so on, can and will benefit from it too. This does not mean you don't care about others. It simply means you have your priorities in order instead of consistently putting the needs of others before your own. The idea is to put yourself in a position to be able to help others without forgetting about you.

Helpful Habits

* Take care of your own emotional needs before anyone else's.

* What makes you who you are? List out all the things you like about yourself.

DAY 28

Today, I am going to reward myself for all the efforts that I have put into my personal development. I feel motivated and ready to face the day. This has become possible because I have consistently made a conscious effort towards my growth and I will treat myself for taking that initiative.

Reward Yourself

"Work diligently. Work hard. Focus. Perform as if you are at the Olympics. One day, unexpectedly, it will start paying off."
– Joan F. Marques

The past 27 days have been all about doing things that will make you feel better about yourself. Hopefully by now, you can already feel a difference mentally, emotionally, physically, and spiritually. I am sure that every day has not been the same. While some may have been a piece of cake, others may have been terrifying and extremely hard on you. Nevertheless, you have come this far and you deserve a reward. Today, reward yourself. That's right; whatever you want, you can have it. Make it something that you will feel like you have worked towards.

The reason you need to reward yourself is because it is very rare that we give ourselves credit for the work that we do to enhance our lives in a positive way. Unless we recognize that we care enough about ourselves to make this happen, we will not feel motivated to continue these efforts. Kudos to you for staying on course and not giving up! You have come this far. Keep going!

Helpful Habits

* All work and no play is no fun. Always have a balance of both!

* The best gifts are often the gifts we give ourselves when we do something to acknowledge how far we have come on our journey.

DAY 29

Today, I feel extremely motivated because of the changes I have
made over the past 28 days. I am committed to continuing to
make positive, necessary changes for my life.

Make a List of Differences You See in Yourself

"Believe in yourself! Have faith in your abilities! Without a humble but reasonable confidence in your own powers you cannot be successful or happy."
– Normal Vincent Peale

You have put in a lot of effort to get to this point. What results do you see in your attitude, physique, and your mental well-being? The difference may lie in the way you feel about yourself, your career, or even your personal life. You may have found a new way to approach bad days when they arise. Or maybe you have found a love for new things that you always wanted to try and have finally incorporated into your schedule. These differences are proof that you are doing the work it takes to continue to grow as a strong woman. Think about and make a list of differences that you have noticed in yourself. If you are able to see these differences, then those around you will be able to see them as well. If you feel like it is a little too hard to make this list on your own, you can get help from your friends and family. Try to list as many things as you can. Make a note of why you feel different and also jot down what you can do to retain these newfound habits. A list of positive changes will boost your confidence. Once you have this list ready, put it in a place where you can see it often.

Helpful Habits

* Always be aware of the things that make you a better woman and do more of whatever that is often.

* Be proud of the woman you are and make room for the woman you are becoming!

DAY 30

Today, when I look in the mirror, I will be reminded to always love, support, and encourage the person who is looking back at me. I will not forget how far I have come on my journey. This is just the beginning of a new, amazing life for me.

Stay Motivated

"Of course motivation is not permanent. But then, neither is bathing; but it is something you should do on a regular basis."
– Zig Ziglar

Motivation is something that you can lose very easily. You have just gone through a month of tedious introspection and change. You are now reaping the benefits of these efforts. Naturally, you are motivated and charged up. But, how long will this excitement phase last? Well, it is entirely up to you. If you are able to stay motivated, you are on your way to greater things! Don't get stuck in a rut or let a bad day here and there deter you or cause you to get off track. Since you got this far, try to keep going another 30 days. Take it one day, one month at a time.

For the past month, you have had something new to look forward to each day. Now that you know the secrets to staying motivated, make your own list. You can start over with Day 1 or you can create your own guide for the next 30 days based on what you've learned. Choose the things that have challenged you the most and continue to use those to build your confidence and self-esteem. If you make up your mind, you can definitely stay motivated. There's nothing stopping you! You can do it!

Helpful Habits

* Live a life full of happiness, love, and purpose.

* Don't be one of those people who gets random sprits of motivation and excitement one minute then slows down and gives up. Be consistent and keep striving towards your goals!

Notes and Ideas

Date: _____

_____

_____

_____

_____

_____

_____

_____

_____

_____

_____

_____

_____

_____

_____

Plan of Action

Date: _____

_____

_____

_____

_____

_____

_____

_____

_____

_____

_____

_____

_____

_____

_____

A Note From the Author

You made it through 30 days of learning to **Trust the Process.** Remember that you can achieve everything that you want to if you put your mind to it. This is not the end of your journey, but instead, the beginning. Keep pushing forward! With all the regularities in life and the responsibilities that we cannot shy away from, it might be hard to remain focused at times. It is natural to feel discouraged and unmotivated, but the challenge is to rise from that low feeling and pull yourself up!

I wish for each of you who has completed the challenges over the last 30 days a wonderful life. I also hope that this book has been successful in shedding some light on the real power and control that you have in your lives. If you feel like you benefitted from this book, I urge you to share the things you learned with others. Finally, I want to say, "thank you" for taking the time to read my book and explore a new awareness of self-elevation. I hope that your life will never be the same and that the words of wisdom I have provided will forever be a blessing. Have fun and keep taking steps of growth toward becoming the woman you were born to be.

Love,

Leanne
xo

Connect with us!
Join the conversation by using the hashtags
#ITrustMyProcess and #TTPbook.

Visit www.officialjonessisters.com
Facebook: www.facebook.com/officialjonessisters
Twitter: @2JonesSisters
Instagram: @TheJonesSisters

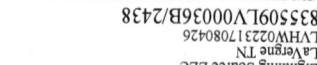